I0177527

# Steps to Successful Home Education

By Christina L. Berry, Ed. D.
Taken from the workshop: Special
Encouragement for Special Needs

One Faith Publishing
A Ministry of the Berry Family

## Books by Christie Berry

*Program Planning and Development*
*Learning Styles and Interests*
*Strengths, Struggles and Strategies*
*Home Made Games for Fun in Learning*
*Hidden Treasures: A Bible Study for Special Moms*

ISBN 978-1-60300-006-2

© 2002 –2011

One Faith Publishing
A Ministry of the Berry Family

Reprint with permission only
One Faith Ministries
PO Box 8391
Huntsville, AL 35808

Scripture Quotations taken from the King James Sacred Name Version.

Cover Design by One Faith Ministries
©2011
All rights reserved

For order information visit:
www.onefaithpub.com

All rights reserved. No part of this book may be reproduced or transmitted in any form or by any means, electronic or mechanical, including photocopying, recording, or by any information storage and retrieval system, without written permission from the author, except for brief quotations in a review with full credit given.

To The Father, who gave me this
word to share with others.
To my Family, who encouraged me to
follow the Spirit's leading.

# Acknowledgements

First and foremost, I would like to thank Yahovah, for giving me the leading and guiding of His Holy Spirit in this work and for giving me the gift of GAB!

Thanks to my family for putting up with me while I put this together long days and late nights.

Special thanks to my mother, Donna, for being my first editor and seeing my roughest drafts and my friend, Cindy, for giving me a 'deadline' so that I could finish what I started and for teasing me when I needed it the most!

Thanks to Cathy, for letting me spend hours in her little shop copying and visiting so that this could get published in the early years.

Thanks to Liz, for her hospitality and understanding when I was up late that night hearing from the Father and *not* visiting with her and her family.

# Contents

# Contents

# Introduction

This message was originally given to me by God the night before I was supposed to speak at a large convention in Montgomery, AL. I had arrived prepared for the first day's workshops and I had all but one presentation for the second day. Friday night I still had no idea what I would share for the final workshop that was to encourage special needs moms and dads that were attending the convention.

We were staying with a wonderful host family that has become our good friends over the years and I explained my dilemma and asked their forgiveness for not spending the evening enjoying their awesome hospitality and company. Of course, they understood and I retreated to a quiet area to seek God. Still very unsure of what I would share, I began looking through my notes and the Word. God began to reveal this presentation, one step at a time. The Holy Spirit moved me smoothly through each step with a new realization and a fresh perspective that I had not seen before in the verses that had been stored in my heart. This has been one of the most important and helpful workshops I have ever given. Many families have been given an audio version of this workshop as a gift to encourage them.

I decided that this message was much too important not to share with a larger audience. So I have put it into a book to make it available to as many as God divinely decides. We are also looking at producing an audio CD. Please share this book and let the ripples of God's Word touch lives far and wide.

Blessings,
Christie Berry

# Pray for Guidance

**Eph 5:17** *"Wherefore be ye not unwise, but understanding what the will of Elohim is."*

Although this seems simplistic and obvious, it will not come as a surprise that many truly do not understand what the will of the Lord is! This is especially true for those seeking God's direction for their children. Spiritual guidance, academics, special activities... what is important to God? What about Discipling, Training, Shepherding, Guiding? Where is the balance?

We are responsible to understand God's will for ourselves and our children in as much as He reveals it to us. God does not call you to do something He has not prepared you to do. But the preparation comes with seeking Him, and through His revelation to you as you seek. He will prepare you and give you all the tools and abilities you need to teach your child. You were chosen to parent the child you have and God will not leave you alone to figure it out! He HAS equipped YOU to be the Parents of the children He has given to you. He does not make mistakes!

Imagine if I were to whisper very faintly, "If you can't hear me, get closer." You would get closer so you didn't miss what was being said. Now, imagine, again, if I were to whisper several times, quieter than before, "If you can't hear me, get closer." Each time you move closer and closer until you could hear me well. Moving closer to someone in order to hear them is the natural thing to do.

***If you can't hear Him, get closer!***

*"Draw nigh unto God, and He will draw nigh to you"* **James 4:8a**

God gives us all the tools and guidance we need to bring up our children with and without disabilities. We are equipped! Seek God daily so that you can know what to do, what to say, and how to teach!

### Ps 25:4-10

*"Show me thy ways, O YHVH; teach me thy paths. Lead me in thy truth, and teach me: for thou art the Elohim of my salvation; on thee do I wait all the day. Remember, O YHVH, thy tender mercies and thy loving kindnesses; for they have been ever of old. Remember not the sins of my youth, nor my transgressions: according to thy mercy remember thou me for thy goodness' sake, O YHVH. Good and upright is the*

*YHVH: therefore will He teach*
*sinners in the way. The meek will He*
*guide in justice: and the meek will*
*He teach his way. All the paths of*
*YHVH are mercy and truth unto such*
*as keep his covenant and his*
*testimonies."*

Pray and ask God to show you His ways. We need to pray, we need to be disciplined, we need to press toward the mark, and sometimes, we need to cry out to God! That's ok! God knows your hurt and your heart. He did not leave you alone. He equips us with all that we need to press toward Him, to be disciplined, and to teach our children. He has not left you alone. His mercy and grace shall follow you. His mercy and grace are enough for you!

**"But how do I hear Him?"** You might ask.
That is a very good question! Let's see what He says about hearing His voice.

In 1 Kings 19, Elijah believes he is the only prophet left in the world and Jezabel is out to kill him! (Do we recognize that feeling of being the only one? I know I did!) So, as the story goes, Elijah pleads to God to take his life. (God, get us out of this situation! I can't do this!) God leads him to a cave at Mount Horeb and tells him to stand at the mouth of the cave. God sends a great wind, an earthquake, and fire and tells Elijah that He is not in the wind, earthquake or fire. Then God speaks with a still small voice and Elijah realizes that this is the voice of the Creator!

There is a still small voice speaking to us all the time, yet the wind, earthquakes and fires keep our attention away from it. Sometimes it is just a whispering thought. The noises, activities, and emergencies that fill our days are constantly distracting us from the still small voice, the guidance that the Father is trying to give. The enemy enjoys keeping us from hearing from the Father. Many times he sparks the fires and sets up distractions to lure us away from our Father. Learn to pick your battles, learn to let the fires burn themselves out. Listen to the Father, He will tell you which fires, which activities and emergencies need your attention and which ones can be left for Him to handle. Listen for the still small voice. It takes practice to know when it is God talking and not our own minds and thoughts. Start with the little things and be faithful in them and you will grow to know how to hear Him in the big things. I suggested to one young mom that she should pray about what to wear each day, listen and be obedient. God would show her when she was hearing from Him. So she tried listening to Him regarding her daily attire. Much to her surprise, every time she wore clothes that she wouldn't have picked for herself (you know the blouse that hangs in the closet that you never wear) many people that day would comment on the outfit or specific item that He told her to wear! She came to visit one day and told me how this had happened over and over. She was amazed that

God cared about what she wore. I explained that He cares about everything about us, but more importantly, He wants us to learn to hear Him, listen to Him, wait on Him and be obedient to Him. She learned a valuable lesson on how to hear from the Father! Try it for yourself, learn to hear His still small voice. It is imperative for your home school journey and the education of your child.

# Press

**Phil 3:14** *"I press toward the mark for the prize of the high calling of God in Messiah Yeshua"*

When you are at the end of your rope *don't* tie a knot and hang on! Let go and let God! He will carry you when you let Him, when we come to the end of ourselves. That's when He is strongest! That's when His miracles can happen!

When I finished college, many years ago, the story around the public school was that the 'life span' of a special education teacher (how long they teach before they totally burn out) was about

7 years. Recently, while talking with a local therapist friend, she informed me that the 'life span' for a special education teacher in the public system is only 2 years! If we look at the fact that "they" (the public system teachers) only have our special needs children for 7 hours a day, 5 days a week, 9 months a year, then, those of us that are home educating our special needs child 24 hours a day, 7 days a week, should be totally burned out by the end of our first school year. That's about 9 months! God gets us to the end of ourselves quickly so He can step in and take over! Let Him!!! His will is always best for us.

But, we are not just by-standers in the discipling of our children. We are disciples! We are in the Army of God! Let's look at the discipline of the Army; Get up and out of bed at 3:00 am, dressed and ready to move out at the first instruction, primed for our mission. How many of you would be willing to get up at 3 am? How many would want to? As disciples, we don't always like the instruction, or the discipline, but we know it is necessary. Are we disciplined enough to do our mission? Are we willing to make changes in ourselves to meet the needs of our children? Are we willing to do what we don't feel like doing? That's what a disciple does; discipline's himself to carry out the Lord's instruction!

Take time to listen and learn from God. Press yourself to reach the mark God has called you to do. He equips *you*, not the special education teacher, not the therapist, *you.* He will teach and lead you in everything and in every direction needed to teach your child, to fulfill your mission. He didn't make a mistake. He created you and your child. Don't grow weary in well doing. Let Him carry the yoke.

# Learn from God

**Mt 11:28** *"Come unto me, all ye that labor and are heavy laden, and I will give you rest."*

This verse is so profound for such few words. First it says, "Come to me." Learn from me. Let me scrape out your brain of all the presuppositions of our culture and ideas and throw it away, because our brains are full of man's ways not God's ways. He wants to refill your mind with His way of doing things. But, remember, His ways are foolish in the eyes of man, thus the new ideas may seem foolish or may not be what others are doing.

Then, it says, "I will give you rest." Only then,

when you have come to Him, learned from Him, will you have rest and contentment with the labor to which you have been called by God to do! His burden is light. He will carry the greatest portion.

When training a young ox, a farmer uses a stronger ox to carry the weight of the large yoke. The yoke that is upon the younger ox is there to guide him to learn direction, commands, and instruction. This way the younger ox only felt the yoke turn him or bring him along and he never bore the weight of it. This is the way God's yoke is, He carries the weight and we only feel the guidance of the yoke, never its weight. If we are trying to carry it on our own, we are not allowing the Lord to carry it for us! If it feels heavy, ask the Lord to carry the heavy load for you. He will!

As I mentioned earlier, God's ways are foolish in the eyes of man. Let's see what His word says:

### 1 Corinthians 1:25-26

*"Because the foolishness of God is wiser than men; and the weakness of God is stronger than men. For ye see your calling, brethren, how that not many wise men after the flesh, not many mighty, not many noble, are called."*

We learn from God. He teaches us how to teach our children and it may seem foolish to others and to ourselves. Moms you already know your ministry, first to your husband and then your children. Many wise men do not know their calling or purpose, they don't have a clue! How far ahead is the one whom God has called and they are aware of their calling!

### 1 Corinthians 1:27 *But God*

*hath chosen the foolish things of the world to confound the*

*wise; and God hath chosen
the weak things of the world
to confound the things which
are mighty; And base things
of the world, and things which
are despised, hath God
chosen, yea, and things which
are not, to bring to naught
things that are.*

### But God

This is His word, *But God*. It reminds me that He fills in all the holes that I can't fill myself. He carries the heaviest of burdens, the largest of yokes. There is no mission too large to accomplish when God has sent me out! He does the same for you! He confounds the wise and uses the weak things to confound the mighty! We are the weak things that confound the wise! All the wisdom of the professionals, teachers, therapists, we confound them all! God uses the weird, strange, base things, and His foolishness to confound the wise. Let Him scrape out your brain and let Him fill it with the tools that you need to learn His foolish ways and you will be equipped to teach your children! You are equipped to train up and shepherd your child!

# Do What Works for You

**Deut 6:6-7** *"And these words, which I command thee this day, shall be in thine heart: And thou shalt teach them diligently unto thy children, and shalt talk of them when thou sittest in thine house, and when thou walkest by the way, and when thou liest down, and when thou risest up".*

Now, let's read this again... "And these words, which I command thee this day, shall be taught by rote for 2 hours of repetition while sitting at the table perfectly still without a break. And thou shalt teach them diligently unto thy children, by reading about them in expensive text books that are used most often in the homeschooling community. Ye shall teach them while sitting at the table, when thou wakest up and continuing until the 6th hour!"

OK! Enough joking around! When we first start out we only know one way to teach; how we were taught. We have the mess in our heads that man has put there. What we need to do is scrape it out! Don't bring the public school home. The wisdom of man is foolish to God. Likewise, the wisdom of God confounds the wise man. Every moment of every day we should be teaching God's wisdom and shepherding our child's heart. This isn't a burden, it is a joyful time. It's a time of courting your child's heart and shepherding him as He grows. Lead the child as the yoke leads the young ox. Let the child work side by side with us, together we can learn perseverance, patience, loving kindness, and the fruit of the Spirit!

Children might be able to recite all the fruit of the Spirit, but most adults can't live it yet! We try! I know I'm learning a lot of patience through my children! But remember tribulation teaches patience! (So, now you know what it's like at my home!)

Use a relaxed, structured approach, unit studies, Charlotte Mason, Child-chosen Learning, call it what you may, but make sure you teach them! We have to help them, lead them, teach them, just as God is teaching us with a light yoke, when we talk, when we sit, and when we walk together. Sometimes we find ourselves repeating the same things over and over again. Many times it is necessary to go in circles. You may also find yourself going in circles if your child has not gained the maturity level needed to grasp the information. Teaching the same things again and again teaches perseverance both to our children and to us. Pressing toward that mark!

Remember that God has created your holy family! Learning from your children can help you learn from God. By putting your children before yourself, denying yourself, and treating them better than yourself as it says in Philippians chapter 2, is a great lesson of God we can learn from our children.

# Be Flexible AND Structured

**1 Timothy 5:13** *"And withal they learn to be idle, wandering about from house to house; and not only idle, but tattlers also and busybodies, speaking things which they ought not."*

Although this verse is speaking of idle women... it applies to our children as well. Are they tattlers and busybodies? Do they speak things they ought not? This is the bread of idleness spoken of in Proverbs 31. It is much better to keep them busy with structure and productivity.

Here is a simple list to help you be flexible and structured:

## Structure

Our children need structure or they will miss the basic skills they need to progress. We need structure both in our goals for the month and year, and in our daily routine. Children with disabilities will not just 'get it' most of the time. Specific steps toward a goal are necessary and will help the child reach their full potential and grow toward their purpose. A daily routine is important to help children know what is expected of them. It allows for shepherding and discipling.

## Self-guidance

Of course, we want to teach toward self-guidance, but don't expect it to be perfect. Many of our children can't self-guide. Shelly, my youngest, would much rather be watching Barney all day long, than do anything different. The Word of God tells us that it is our human sin nature to be lazy!

Don't allow your children to become lazy.

## Productivity

Help your child learn to be productive. Now this is an interesting topic. What is 'productive'? You will have to ask yourselves and seek God to determine what will be considered productive in your home. In our home, television is only productive if it is educational in nature and is limited in time and topic. But, doing chores, working on note booking, sewing, scrap booking, practicing for an upcoming event, washing clothes, helping one another, and outdoor play for our younger children are considered productive. We do not require constant productivity throughout the day, only during certain parts of our schedule. This allows freedom within the parameters of our structure and in our daily schedule.

## Group Time

As often as possible shepherd your sheep in a group. Teach in a multilevel approach or unit study. Read to them, play with them, learn their interests, let them teach you something they have learned, scrap book together, watch an educational video or television show, play an educational game. There are many ways to teach your children as a group.

## Block Schedule

A block schedule is choosing to work on a specified subject such as a unit study on animals for a set period of time and then switching to a unit study on American History for the next block of time usually a semester. This is very flexible, you can block days of the week if you want to do a day of math, a day of science, and a day of reading. You may choose any combination as a block of instruction that fits your family and situation best.

## Individual Work (to do list)

I give my kids a 'to do' list that they are to complete for the day. Usually, for the youngest it is pictures or simple words that I read to her so she knows what will be done for the next hour, or 3 hours, depending on what is happening that day. For my teens I write them a more extensive list and in the priority I would like to see them done. This gives them something to refer back to and allows them to be as independent as possible still within the framework of structure. Sometimes I add an amount of time for each activity (this helps them see an end to the work, or keeps them from spending all day on one activity when other things need to be done) I include productive time on the list so they can choose something they want to do. Sometimes, I have to put a few suggestions on the productive time so that they can make good choices.

Help your children learn to find things to keep them busy. Turn off the TV and video games for a week and help them learn to play with a purpose! It is amazing how our children grow before our eyes when we lead and guide them within a framework that is recommended by the Creator of the Universe!

# Decide What is Important

**Prov 4:5,7** *"Get wisdom, get understanding: forget it not; neither decline from the words of my mouth...Wisdom is the principal thing; therefore get wisdom: and with all thy getting get understanding."*

I can't tell anyone what is important or productive for their home. You will have to rely on God to let you know your child's purpose and to give you guidance as to what is important and productive. He knows what is important and what you need to do to train your child. My daily goal is to have time with Him even if nothing else gets done for the day, 'life happens'! Lord, help us get wisdom and understanding in your will, your word, and your way!

Sometimes we have to teach things that are difficult for the child. There are things we just have to do, like reading! So learn your child's behavior of resistance and frustration. There is a difference between not wanting to do something and becoming frustrated because is it very difficult. Most of us can pick up on our child's behavior. You know what I'm talking about, that look, the clinched hands, or giving up. What I recommend is what Sharon Hensley calls the 'one more' rule. This is when your child is showing resistance to continuing with the work at hand. Tell them that they need to do one more (and then one more if it is appropriate) until you identify if the behavior is resistance or frustration. If they are frustrated, then you stop. This teaches them that they can't just give up and to persevere and work hard even when it isn't easy. It will also help you identify the difference between your child's frustration level and resistance.

There are times when the resistance is actually rebellion. If you suspect that the resistance is rebellion, it is time to seek the Father for how best to work on the heart issue of rebellion. Remember to look at yourself first, because we can only change ourselves and how we act, react and respond. We can't change our children, only the Heavenly Father can do that! Pray for wisdom.

# What is Success?

**Joshua 1:8** *This book of the law shall not depart out of thy mouth; but thou shalt meditate therein day and night, that thou mayest observe to do according to all that is written therein: for then thou shalt make thy way prosperous, and then thou shalt have good success.*

You will have to decide what Success means to you as well. Is success a college diploma? Is that a realistic goal for each of your children? How about learning a trade or starting an apprenticeship with someone in a small business. Is being independent a choice of success for your child? What about their Spiritual well being, is it at the top of the list of what success is?

**Pr 9:10** *The fear of the YHVH is the beginning of wisdom: and the knowledge of the holy is understanding.*

**Pr 24:14** *So shall the knowledge of wisdom be unto thy soul: when thou hast found it, then there shall be a reward, and thy expectation shall not be cut off.*

For our family success is our Spiritual growth and well being. God will equip our children for their mission if we work on His plan for their lives. Of course, we work on the important academic areas, (I call them the "4 R's" Readin', 'ritin', 'rithmatic, and religion.) As we seek the knowledge of wisdom and the Father, we gain the success He gives us.

## Pr 2:1-9

*My son, if thou wilt receive my words, and hide my commandments with thee; So that thou incline thine ear unto wisdom, and apply thine heart to understanding; Yea, if thou criest after knowledge, and liftest up thy voice for understanding. If thou seekest her as silver, and searchest for her as for hid treasures; Then shalt thou understand the fear of the YHVH, and find the knowledge of God. For YHVH giveth wisdom: out of his mouth cometh knowledge and understanding. He layeth up sound wisdom for the righteous: He is a buckler to them that walk uprightly. He keepeth the paths of judgment, and preserveth the way of his saints. Then shalt thou understand righteousness, and judgment, and equity; yea, every good path.*

Ask God to define success for your home, family, and each individual. God created us all uniquely and we are to reach His goal for our lives. Anoint your children in the Word of God, like the oil that ran down Aaron's beard. Allow God's anointing to grow them and bloom them into the successes He would have them to be. You are the appointed missionary to your children. It is your responsibility to lead them in the way they should go.

# Take Time to De-Stress

**Phil 4:6-7** *"Be careful for nothing; but in every thing by prayer and supplication with thanksgiving let your requests be made known unto God. And the peace of God, which passeth all understanding, shall keep your hearts and minds through Messiah Yeshua."*

Be careful for nothing. Other translations use the word anxious. Anxiety is how we feel when we are overwhelmed, feeling burned out, or trying to carry the weight of the yoke. But God promises what He will do here in Philippians if we are obedient, keep from anxiety, and bring all things to Him with thanksgiving. He promises He will give us peace.

But what about all the work we need to do? "We are behind!" Behind what? The couch? Who's schedule are you on? Man's or God's? How can you be behind God's plan?

Let's look at an annual plan for a family home educating a special needs child:

| Therapeutic | Academics | Independence |
|---|---|---|
| Perception<br>Processing<br>Physical<br>Occupational<br>Speech/Language<br>Therapy<br>Attention | Language Arts<br>Math<br>Social Studies<br>Science<br>Bible<br>PE | Self-help Skills<br>Behavior<br>Social Skills<br>Vocational Skills<br>Study and<br>Organizational<br>Skills |

This is a three part list of what most parents home educating children with disabilities need to consider when creating a program plan. If you were to cover up the first and last column you will see what a typical child works on for their 'school' day. Looking at the whole chart, it is easy to become overwhelmed thinking of how to get through it all. God will tell you what to work on. Sometimes He will reveal what needs work through the behavior of the child. But remember, His yoke is light, if you are feeling overwhelmed you are trying to do His job! Remember 1 Corinthians 1:25 God's wisdom will seem foolish and Philippians 3:14 press toward the mark.

Think about your child when they wanted so badly to help you. Remember them jumping in to help and making a mess of what you were working on? The intent of their heart was pure, but they didn't wait for instructions before they jumped in! We do the same thing with God. When we see what He is doing we want to help Him and jump in without any instruction and we end up making a mess of things. This leads us to stress and anxiety. God uses you to shepherd and disciple your child, God has equipped you! Wait for His instruction. However, sometimes we are tired. Even Messiah went up the mountain to get away from the people to refresh (or de-stress). It will be important for you to find rest time away from your children. Consider carefully your quiet place and time. It is NOT restful or refreshing when I go in my room for some alone with God time. Why? Well, I hear my dear husband fussing at the kids. I hear my kids screaming, "DAD!!!" This is NOT de-stressing! Let's face it, my dear husband does things differently than I do. He chooses his battles differently, he disciples differently. Needless to say, sometimes we have to find ourselves a place ... AWAY! Or, we can find a place to send our children.

This place for our children is called respite care. Funding for respite is not always available. So respite may be daddy taking the children to the library, or a friend taking them to the park while you stay at home. When I was living in Germany a friend of mine and I swapped kids! I know that may sound strange, but actually it worked well.

We actually swapped babysitting. She watched my child 4 hours on Tuesday and I watched her child 4 hours on Thursday.  It worked out really well! Pray that God lead you to the right person to give you occasional respite care. You may have to teach a helper how to deal with your child's issues, pray with them, learn about them, bond with the person. You may be able to find a mom's day out that will take your special needs child and give you time for an appointment at the spa or what ever you need. Also, look for support groups. Many times you will find another mom that can help you out once in a while.

**Other ideas for de-stressing:**

- Kidnap a friend!
- Exercise (getting up a little early, yeah that's discipline! I walk the pasture when I am disciplined enough to do it.)
- Read or listen to something humorous (my son does that for me!)

- Keep a calendar:   We keep a 3 month out calendar for everyone to see. This keeps my teen from over booking me. Now, if I can just stop over booking myself, I'll have it made!
- Take a weekly 'Mom's Day Off'.
Use the time to finish the many projects that are sitting in the closet: sewing, writing, relaxing, reading.

Most of all, seek God, He will tell you where to find opportunities for respite care!

# Grab the Teachable Moment

**Proverbs 4:13** *"Take fast hold of instruction; let her not go: keep her; for she is thy life."*

Proverbs tells us to grasp, grab, hold onto Godly instruction and not let it go. It is through holding fast to that instruction that will give us life. Make every moment count, make every moment a teachable moment. Deuteronomy 6:6 says to teach this Godly instruction when we walk, sit and lay down.

When we moved to the country years ago, we learned of a trash pick-up date in which the county would pick up trash at the side of the road.

Well, the first time the county came by our home everything came to a screeching halt! A large dump truck and a truck with a huge claw stopped at our pile of trash and we watched intently as they picked up the trash. Now, you would be amazed what types of discussions can come out of watching a claw pick up trash! We discussed machinery, recycling, careers, the difference between trash and garbage (not that I *really* understand that concept yet, it's definitely a new one for me), well you get the picture! Grab any teachable moment.

A few years back we cared for Satch's aging grandmother. We learned about selflessness, compassion, service, and disease. When she passed away we learned about death, dying, and what happens after we die. It was a difficult year, but we took the moment to learn even in the most difficult times.

Hold fast, grab every moment you can to teach

your children about life! Teach them about God, family, faith, and you may want to throw in math and reading along the way, too!

# Expect Difficult Days

**James 1:2-3**

> *"My brethren, count it all joy when ye fall into divers temptations. Knowing this, that the trying of your faith worketh patience."*

**1Th 5:18** *"In every thing give thanks: for this is the will of God in The Messiah concerning you."*

Expect difficult days, they will come! We are admonished to count it all joy when there are difficult times. It is so hard to count difficult times as joy. I look at Peter, when he stepped out of the boat and began to walk toward Messiah on the water. He walked on the water perfectly well until he began to look at the dire circumstances around him! He took his eyes off the only one that could help his walk and looked to the storm that was raging around him. It hurts when your faith is being stretched and pulled like a rubber band waiting to snap. Yet, this is exactly what God wants and expects us to do! Let our faith stretch, know that He can do all things and get us through the stretching and let our faith grow no matter how much it hurts!

It becomes difficult to see Messiah in the storm of our circumstances. Just as Peter took his eyes off of the Lord, so we find ourselves looking at the circumstances rather than the One who can keep us in His bosom safe from those outside interferences. Of course, we need to remember as we go through the storm, God promises to carry us through the storm, but He never said we won't get wet! But sometimes we struggle to get away from God and do our own thing (or help Him out). This reminds me of catching one of our cats before it gets to the road and in danger of traffic.

It struggles to free itself from my arms, to run away unaware that it is in my arms it will be safe. We struggle with God to run from the circumstances around us, when He wants to hold us in His arms near His heart and keep us safe from it all.

Even when God gives us all the things we have talked about in this little book, the difficult days still come! But don't count them as lost. I heard someone say that we should expect impossible days. I say nothing is impossible when you stay in God's will. We need to reclaim those difficult days! Count them all joy! Turn the stumbling block that Satan has put in your path into a stepping stone! Look at what was accomplished for the day. Learn how a family pulls together in times of difficulty or crisis. Take the opportunity to learn hospitality, patience, and flexibility. Use the opportunity to display your understanding and ability to be flexible to the children. Pattern or model how to handle stressful times. Believe me the children are looking! Is mom having a tough day? Ask them to pray with you. Pray that God help you. Give the situation over to God. Seek out the Word of God and find a reference that speaks to you in your time of trouble. Modeling this to your children will teach them volumes that you could otherwise only talk about and hope they catch a hold of.

# Let your Child Dream

**Ephesians 1:11** *"In whom also we have obtained an inheritance, being predestinated according to the purpose of Him who worketh all things after the counsel of His own will"*

Each person has been predestined with a specific purpose here on this earth. As we grow and seek God's will He begins to reveal that will and purpose in our lives. Our experiences help us to grow, strengthen our faith and eventually fulfill that purpose. Just as each of us has a purpose, each of our children is predestined with a purpose as well. As our children learn, experience, grow, and dream, God's will is slowly being revealed. We can also ask God's will and purpose for our children. As God's purpose is being revealed we can encourage and teach them to seek His will and strive toward their purpose.

I heard a story once of a 10 year old girl that wanted to be a ballerina. She had dreamed most of her life of becoming a ballerina and dancing on a stage with other ballerinas. She begged her mother to buy her ballet shoes, to take her to the ballet, to help her reach her dream, but her mother would always tell her no. Her mother would say, "Stop day dreaming and be realistic. You will never be able to do that!" dashing her daughters dreams with each word that spewed from her tongue. You see, the girl had cerebral palsy and spent most of her day in a wheel chair. But her dream was real! God had placed in her a passion! She would dance with her chair in the living room while watching ballet on the television.

What is your child's passion? Does he day dream

or spend hours playing in a manner that could reveal his purpose, talents and abilities? If we don't let our children dream, they will not have the opportunity to expose their passions and find their true purpose. Helping our children find where they fit into the world and what God's purpose is in their lives is a very important gift to give your child. Our children have a predestined calling, a purpose, ordained by God to complete the mission He calls them to do. Letting them dream helps them find that purpose.

I was ministering at a conference one time and a family approached my booth and asked me what kind of purpose God could have for their four year old daughter that functioned at a six month old level. She was their youngest child of four children. I was on the spot. I prayed a quick and quiet prayer, "God, now what do I say?" The words that He gave me were hard to hear, but had great truth. His words were, "If all she can be is the Godly sandpaper that smoothes out your rough edges, then she is fulfilling that purpose wonderfully! If she is able to help your older children to be loving and kind to others with disabilities, learn to be caregivers, helpers to one another, she is completing her mission." This message may be difficult for some of us to hear, but truth sometimes hurts. Let your 'Godly sandpaper' work on you!

## Learn to Advocate

**Ezekiel 22:29-30** *"The people of the land have used oppression, and exercised robbery, and have vexed the poor and needy: yea, they have oppressed the stranger wrongfully. And I sought for a man among them, that should make up the hedge, and stand in the gap before me for the land, that I should not destroy it: but I found none."*

Who will stand in the gap for the children? Who has God put in their lives to intercede and protect them? Of course, the family has the responsibility to advocate to the Father on behalf of the children He has given us. To make up the hedge, to protect, to keep them from the people of the land that oppress, rob and vex. We are called by God as parents to stand in the gap for our children. We are also called to teach them to advocate for themselves; to know the will of the Father; to stand on His precepts in the midst of the storms.

Help your children to find their purpose. Help them to find resources to benefit their purpose. Know your child's needs and find ways and means to meet those needs. Teach your child how to find ways to meet their own needs. Teach them to depend on God for their weaknesses. Teach them to seek Him for strength and comfort in the Holy Spirit. Ask God to provide Christian professionals that can help them as adults reach their full potential. Stand boldly at the throne of Grace and ask God for mercy and help in time of need. Teach your child boldness in Messiah to give him the ability to be his own mouthpiece to speak the things he has need of. Teach him to have faith that God will provide above and beyond all he can ask or think. (See Ephesians 3:20)

We stand in the gap. We teach them diligently as we go out, as we walk along the path. God will honor that work that we do on behalf of our children, but we must also help them to rely on Him and stand up for what they know is right. Teach them that they may fail, but to persevere and reach for the mark for themselves. They can do it, you can show them how by your example.

# Be a Super Sleuth

**Be a Super Sleuth for your child.**

· Pray for Guidance: Seek God for guidance daily.

· Press: Press on toward the calling for which you are chosen, and press for your child's purpose.

· Learn From God! Take on His light yoke and learn to follow Him in every step.

· Do What Works for You: Ask God what learning should look like in your home.

· Be Flexible and Structured: Keep a daily routine and set goals for the month and year.

· Decide What is Important: Seek God diligently for what to teach your child.

· Define Success: Entreat God to show you what will be success for each of your children.

· Take Time to De-Stress: Don't let anxiety drag you down.

· Grab the Teachable Moment: Look at each moment as a time to learn and shepherd your child's heart.

· Expect Difficult Days: In everything give thanks.

· Let Your Child Dream: Let them find their Godly purpose.

· Learn to Advocate: Intercede for your children and teach them to advocate for themselves.

# ABC's To Remember

Appropriate goals and curriculum: Find appropriate goals and curriculum

Balance: Create a balanced daily diet of learning difficulties and successes

Consistency: Be consistent with your decisions

Don't Argue: Don't argue; it causes stress and exhaustion

Expectations: Keep your expectations realistic

Frustration vs. resistance: Learn the difference between frustration and resistance in your child (1 more rule to get past the resistance point)

Get Real! Court your child's heart and encourage him to reach God's potential, purpose and mission!

www.ingramcontent.com/pod-product-compliance
Lightning Source LLC
Chambersburg PA
CBHW071634040426
42452CB00009B/1614